A COLLECTION OF POEMS ON SEXUAL AND GENDER BASED VIOLENCE IN LOVING MEMORY OF KEREN-HAPPUCH AONDODOO AKPAGHER AND SEVERAL OTHER VICTIMS

Tears From The Grave

LEMMY UGHEGBE

TEARS FROM THE GRAVE

ISBN: 978-978-799-523-5

 All Bible quotations are taken from the King James Version of the Bible unless otherwise stated.

FOR INFORMATION
Lemmy Ughegbe
Email: lughegbe@gmail.com
Tel: +234 (0) 806-971-6645

PUBLISHED & PRINTED BY

ZENGARY PUBLISHING
40 Sharps Court, Cooks Way, Hitchin
Email: zengaryprinthouse@gmail.com
Tel:+234(0)803-563-1504;+44 (0) 777-109-7728
www.zengaryglobal.com

DEDICATION

To Miss Keren-Happuch Aondodoo Akpagher,
Whose life was cut short by a killer-rapist.

To the Survivors,
Whose resilience paints the canvas of this narrative,
Whose stories echo in the halls of our collective consciousness,
Whose courage lights the way for a brighter, safer tomorrow.

This book is dedicated to you — the unsung heroes of endurance and hope.

May your voices be heard, your pain acknowledged, and your strength celebrated.

In memory of Keren-Happuch Aondodoo Akpagher, whose light may have dimmed but whose spirit shines on in our quest for justice.

And to all those who have stood against the shadows of silence, your bravery inspires us to dismantle the walls of indifference.

Lemmy Ughegbe
Author and Advocate

ACKNOWLEDGEMENTS

In crafting this narrative of resilience and advocacy, I am indebted to a tapestry of individuals and entities, whose unwavering support have been the cornerstone of this endeavour.

First and foremost, my heartfelt gratitude goes to Keren's mother, Vivien Vihimga Akpagher, who felt free enough to express her vulnerability and grief to me. Thank you for trusting me to hold your hands and walk with you; for telling me so much story of Keren that I came to know her so much. This collection was inspired by these experiences. I won't leave you as you continue to take baby steps towards healing.

Special thanks to the survivors — the brave souls who entrusted me with their stories. Your resilience and courage are the driving force behind these pages, and your voices are the heartbeat of change.

To the Men Against Rape Foundation and the Make A Difference Initiative teams, your dedication and tireless efforts in combating sexual and gender-based violence are the backbone of this work. Together, we stand as beacons of hope and catalysts for transformation.

A sincere thank you to the countless organisations and individuals championing the cause of justice, transparency, and healing. Your collaborations and alliances are the threads weaving a stronger, more compassionate fabric for our society.

I extend my appreciation to the readers – the advocates, the empathisers, and those seeking understanding. Your engagement in this dialogue is a pivotal step towards a world free from the shackles of violence.

To my family and my small circle of friends, your unwavering support and encouragement have been my anchor. You've stood by me in the storm, and for that, I am profoundly grateful.

Lastly, this work is dedicated to the memory of Keren-Happuch Aondodoo Akpagher. May her legacy serve as a guiding light in our pursuit of justice and a future where no one walks alone in the shadows of silence.

Lemmy Ughegbe
Author and Advocate

FOREWORD

A Symphony of Voices

In the quiet corridors of grief, you stepped into the shadows with me - a grieving mother, becoming my natural therapist, friend, and confidant. Through this odyssey of sorrow, you wove yourself into the fabric of my emotions and thoughts, becoming a silent companion to my anguish. You transcended the role of a mere activist seeking justice; you became the echo of my pain and a source of solace.

Playing football with Keren's little brother and just being there for us all — you navigated every space to dismantle barriers, to set hearts free. In becoming each of us and all of us, you discovered the tapestry of voices that would shape this collection of poems. This is the outcome of a poignant symphony of emotions of victims, survivors, their families, societies relived and told by the poet. It unfolds how the poet became a grieving mother, bereaved brothers, an advocate, and others.

I therefore invite you into the realm curated by the indomitable Lemmy Ughegbe — not just a poet, but a maestro orchestrating change. His narrative doesn't dwell in the ivory towers or distant realms of theory; it echoes on the front lines of societal struggles. The battle against Sexual and Gender-Based Violence (SGBV) isn't ink on paper; it's etched in the lived experiences eternally engraved on the canvas of reality.

This book isn't a mere compilation; it's a symphony of stories, an opus of insights weaving the tapestry of Ughegbe's life's commitment. Through the Men Against Rape Foundation and the Make A Difference Initiative, you've crafted sanctuaries for healing, understanding, and empowerment.

Prepare to traverse narratives that defy the ordinary – stories that peel back the layers of trauma, courage, and the unyielding spirit of those refusing to be silenced. Ughegbe's work transcends awareness; it's a clarion call to action, an invitation to stand with him against the pervasive darkness of sexual and gender-based violence.

As you turn these pages, brace yourself for more than words – for actions that resonate in the corridors of justice. Let this be a journey, an awakening, a rallying cry for a world where resilience triumphs, advocacy prevails, and justice breathes as a living reality.

Welcome to a symphony where each word is a resonant step towards change, and each story is a testament to the enduring strength of the human spirit.

Yours Sincerely,

Vivien Vihimga Akpagher

HEAVEN'S CALL

The Princess, serene and once eloquent,
Sips from the cup, her spirit spent,
Whispering words that make no sense,
Her voice lost in a cryptic pretense.

Her mother, with tender love and care,
Ponder over the riddle in the air,
Gazing deep into her daughter's eyes,
Hoping to unveil the truth that lies.

But the cup she lifts, a hollow embrace,
Drinks of emptiness, sorrow's trace,
As each futile sip brings no relief,
Only deepening the clouds of grief.

In hushed tones, her voice does strive,
Uttering sounds that fail to derive
Meaning or solace, a tangled refrain,
Causing her mother's heart to strain.

Uncertain, her mother seeks aid,
Urgently, to the hospital they wade,
Yearning for her child's restoration,
Yet witnessing a new destination.

A realm where sorrow and abuse reside,
Alien lands where peace abide,
Where the Princess finds her final call,
In a heavenly home, beyond the fall.

THE STARTLING DISCOVERY

Through hospital doors, paramedics sweep,
A distressed young soul, caught in anguish deep,
Nurses spring forth, tending to her vital score,
Doctors answer the call, their duty to restore.

To steady her weakened form, they embark,
Infusing life's essence, a lifeline to embark,
A compassionate nurse seeks a catheter's aid,
To ease her discomfort, in this moment frayed.

Beside her, a mother, eyes filled with dread,
Whispering prayers for miracles to spread,
Hoping the healer's touch will banish the strife,
And shield her child from the shadows of life.

The doctor lifts her skirt, with a gentle air,
Puzzled by a discharge, a cause for care,
A rubbery presence accidentally revealed,
Igniting questions for the mystery unsealed.

A sample sent for tests, concealed truth's veil,
Revealing a darkness, a sorrowful trail,
Of dead sperm cells within her fragile frame,
A condom, the grim reminder of the abuser's shame.

BULLIED

How could she keep this hidden, deep within,
The wounds of abuse, silent, unseen?
Why didn't she reveal the name of her pain,
Or share her burden, her heart's heavy strain?
These questions swarm, tormenting my mind,
Lost in a bewildering wonder of emotions confined.

My dear confidante, why were you silenced so?
Why couldn't your voice break through the woe?
The theft of your innocence, a treacherous act,
Bearing the weight of trauma, a daunting pact.
Alone, you endured the pain's haunting might,
A prey to a predator's vile, wicked delight.

Where did I stumble, where did I fail?
Why didn't you your story unveil?
These questions echo, yearning for solace,
Yet answers emerge, in the form of this chorus:
How could she have found words so grave?
Do you grasp the grip a predator ensnares?

Threats of death loom, their victims they bind,
"If you dare speak, your life, I'll unwind."
Such sinister silence, coerced by fear's reign,
Forcing her voice into shadows, in vain.
Can you fathom the depths of her plight?
Have you not felt bullying's bitter bite?

Harassed for demanding justice's quest,
Your spirit unwavering, despite the unrest.
If they could intimidate you from afar,
Secure in your refuge, beyond their bar,
Can you not envision the torment she faced,
From the abuser's relentless savage embrace?

Forced into silence, a silenced soul,
Bullied by her tormentor's brutal control,
Imprisoned by fear, her voice held at bay,
Compelled to endure the abuser's vile buffet.

GIBBERISH

In a haze of gibberish, nonsensical and obscure,
She raises an empty cup, lost in words impure.
To and fro, it dances upon her lips,
Yet the meaning eludes, a mystery grips.

Her actions, once gentle, now marked by violence,
Leaving us bewildered, grappling in silence.
In the hospital's confines, she's medically bound,
The test results unveiled a tale profound.

Sepsis has infiltrated her frail frame,
Weakening immunity, fueling the flame,
Compromising blood sugar, casting delirium's spell,
Unleashing chaos within, where reason fell.

A once eloquent coordinator, respected and revered,
Whose authority her brothers coveted,
Has lost her mojo, her voice a tangled sound,
Gibberish spoken, frustration unbound.

In obeisance to the signals of septicemia's might,
She lashes out, trapped in a frenzied fight,
Forcing doctors her hands and legs to bind
The decomposing latex, the culprit we find.

THE BROKEN CUP

I witness your tears, a river that flows,
Your pain I sense, a heavy burden it bestows.
A shattered heart, pieces strewn apart,
Who wouldn't be broken by such cruel art?

Those in whom you trusted, their betrayal profound,
Emptied your cup, its contents unwound,
Splintering joy, fragments scattered wide,
When God blessed you with Keren's stride.

Her birth, a testament, a cup filled with mirth,
Laughter overflowed, a gift of immeasurable worth.
Entrusting her to their care, a bond of trust,
Only to be met with treachery, an unjust thrust.

They repaid your faith with a vile decree,
Breaking the cup, turning laughter to agony.
But hold on to faith, even in despair's thrall,
For the Lord shall answer, mending it all.

He shall transform your ashes into beauty's embrace,
Wipe away your tears, fear's grip shall efface.
Justice will prevail, her abusers shall face
Calamity their companion, until truth they embrace.

Confessions shall come, their guilt unmasked,
Generations to face calamity, a righteous task.
No evil-doer shall escape, as justice takes its toll,
For those who enable escape, their story unfolds.

Stay strong in the journey, for justice shall reign,
And the broken cup atoned.
In God's time, vindication shall be found,
With healing and restoration, love shall abound.

SOBER REFLECTION

Mother, my twelfth birthday approaches near,
Please, let's celebrate with joy and cheer.
No, my dear Didoo, only milestones we commend,
Twelve is young, there's no need to pretend.

But twelve is significant, don't you recall?
Jesus, at twelve, started his ministry, standing tall.
Such was my daughter, with logic so sound,
Her persuasive arguments, eloquently profound.

Thus, we celebrated, amidst laughter and delight,
Unaware that her celestial journey was in sight.
Little did I know, the ones I entrusted her to,
Would extinguish her light, her candle they blew.

If only the spirits had warned of their intent,
To dim her star, in a cruel moment spent.
If they had revealed the undertaker's guise,
I would have cherished each day, with no goodbyes.

Now, left to mourn, I reflect on the day,
When your presence faded, life turned gray.
Each passing day, a solemn reminder,
Of your departure, my heart's eternal cinder.

MOTHER DEAREST

In the face of danger, a threat to your life,
You carried me within, in times of strife,
To full term, a triumph, a cherished birth,
While battling with death, showing your worth.

The angel of death sought to steal you away,
But for my sake, you fought, come what may,
With strength like Samson, you overcame,
That I may drink of your sweet fountain.

For fourteen years, I was nourished by your side,
In your arms, I found solace, where I could confide,
Your love, a fountain that never ceased to flow,
Kindness, compassion, in every embrace I know.

Our banter, a joy, always ending with your smile,
Calling my name, "Didoooo," in your gentle style,
As I was wheeled away, I treasured every moment,
In your presence, dear mother, I was content.

UNANSWERED QUESTIONS

In the wake of night, my eyes wide awake,
My mind consumed, questions tumultuously quake,
Seeking answers, unravelling the mystery untold,
Yearning to understand, as my thoughts unfold.

The cloud of uncertainty veils my mind,
Unanswered questions, a torment unkind,
My sanity wavers, my peace in shards,
Sleep escapes me, stolen by these discords.

Two years have passed since her untimely end,
Yet sleep eludes me, my heart cannot mend,
For the questions persist, haunting my soul,
Yearning for the police to reveal their role.

Who violated my precious baby girl?
Who inflicted upon Keren-Happuch a cruel whirl?
Who shattered my cup, emptying it with disdain?
Who broke my trust, leaving only pain?

Why? Oh why, does justice remain elusive?
These burning questions, relentless and intrusive,
I seek closure by the truth unveiled,
Until then, my restless heart remains assailed.

SILENCED

Bruised and battered, yet on she trudged,
Aching with each step, pain etched deep,
Her innocence stolen, her spirit crushed,
Silent tears flowing, her secrets she'd keep.

"Why do you weep? Why do you limp?"
Her peers questioned with concern,
But her voice trembled, her words subdued,
For his threat still made her heart quake.

The aggressor's threats echoed in her mind,
A constant reminder of the torment he'd bring,
If she dared to speak, to reveal the truth,
To tell the tale of a caregiver turned terror's king.

His imposing figure loomed in her thoughts,
A menacing presence, a spectre of dread,
He held the power to extinguish her light,
To silence her forever, so her heart feared.

A BROTHER'S ANGUISH

In past tense they speak of her, so distant,
Aunts, uncles, sympathisers, in memory's embrace,
Someone they used to see, now transient,
My sister, whom I still long to face.

My mother weeps, her voice calls out her name,
They try to engage me, but I resist the strain,
Uninterested, disengaged, in this sorrowful game,
Speaking of her in the past tense, it's hard to explain.

How can I say goodbye to my sister so dear,
Believe she's gone, never again to return?
I'll hold on to hope, dispel the looming fear,
For in my heart, her memory will forever burn.

NOW, I KNOW

Mother, they mention Dido's name in past,
As if she's vanished, forever withdrawn,
They coax me to join, but my heart holds fast,
I choose not to speak in the same mournful tone.

I can't utter her name in past's cruel embrace,
It feels like closing a book, ending too soon,
Her story unfolding, a hopeful, tender grace,
Yet now, the pages lie blank under the moon.

I clung to the future, in hope's warm embrace,
Believing she'd return, our lives to restore,
Yet Christmas has come, and she's not in this place,
Her story's been altered, forevermore.

With a heart heavy-laden, the truth I confess,
Her journey's been shortened, ended abruptly,
A story cut short, leaving memories, no less,
Now, I know, she's gone from us, so sadly.

A BRUTE'S LOVE

Her wincing and whimpering,
Ignite his relentless rage,
Each punch, a brutal offering,
A fury few can gauge.

Can this be the same man,
Who pledged love's endless climb?
How love turns into a vile plan,
Inflicting hurt and crime.

What love breeds threats so dire,
To lead one to the grave?
What love becomes a fire,
Devouring, cruel and savage?

Love should be a gentle guide,
In the storm, a steady form,
Not a weapon to deride,
Inflicting pain and harm.

We must unveil this love's disguise,
Expose its true grotesque,
For genuine love does rise,
To heal, uplift, and bless.

FACADE

When his voice rises, a bid to dominate,
In argument's quest, his ego unbounds,
Beware, for his control knows no set date.
When kindness graces only your fate,
While others face his harshness and rebounds,
Beware, for his true self begins to state.

When lavish gifts, your heart do captivate,
But others' suffering, he merely surrounds,
Beware, for superficial generosity's weight.
When soft words to you, he does create,
Yet to others, impatience and harsh sounds,
Beware, his facade may disintegrate.

When masculinity boasts, his intentions innate,
A guise for dominance, control that astounds,
Beware, for purity may not decorate.
In all, trust your instincts, they elucidate,
The signs whisper caution in soft rounds,
True love and respect need no false crate.

TEARS FROM THE GRAVE

In sorrow's depths, your pain, I understand,
My tears mix with the weight of your heart's demand,
Beloved mother, you erred not, don't you see,
Your trust and love you gave to me.

In caregivers' hands, you placed your trust,
Unaware of the darkness, concealed unjust,
Blame not yourself, for their choices, not thine,
You shone with love, so pure and divine.

In this time of grief, overwhelming and vast,
Know that you're not alone, love's arms will last,
Embrace solace offered, let healing commence,
May their love guide you to peace, recompense.

From my grave, let tears transform and ignite,
A beacon of strength, through sorrow's darkest night,
Towards hope and renewal, a healing embrace,
As you soak yourself in HIS abiding grace.

BROKEN PROMISE

In the shadowed realm of betrayal's echo,
A promise shattered, trust in fragments strown,
How could guardians turn to cruel tormentors?
Why pledge to care with hearts in darkness sewn?

It's a bitter truth, a harsh reality to face,
Sometimes trust's refuge turns to a haunted space,
Wolves masked as sheep, concealed in their embrace,
Leaving us wounded, questioning their grace.

Dear one, know the fault is not yours to bear,
Their actions mirror their own moral despair,
The broken promise whispers of their own affair,
Their betrayal echoes the darkness they wear.

Though pain may linger, and scars run deep,
Hold to the truth, your spirit they cannot keep,
Time will mend wounds, your strength will steep,
To reclaim your power, their deceit to sweep.

Let not their actions define your inner light,
Within you, a resilient spirit takes flight,
Rise above promises shattered in the night,
Your worth transcends their shallow plight.

Find solace in the love by your side,
Those who see your beauty, your strength, your pride,
Though care's promise by them was denied,
You'll rise, heal, and on solid ground abide.

SHATTERED DREAM

Oh, shattered dreams, so cruelly torn apart,
By the hands of evil, a despicable act.
Your innocent hopes, now tainted and marred,
By a heartless act that left you deeply scarred.

But know, dear one, that your dreams still live,
For within your spirit, strength will give.
Though the path is dark, and tears may fall,
Your light will guide you through it all.

Evil may have cast its shadow on your youth,
But it cannot erase your intrinsic truth.
You are more than a victim of their vile deed,
You're a survivor, a fighter, with the strength you need.

Embrace the power within to heal and mend,
For your dreams endure, they shall not end.
Through the pain, reclaim your might,
And rise above the darkness, into the light.

Seek comfort in those who offer you care,
For love and support will help repair.
Together we stand, united and strong,
To rewrite the future, where dreams belong.

Though the scars may linger, and memories haunt,
Your spirit perseveres, and it shall daunt,
The evil that tried to steal your dreams,
For hope and courage flow in limitless streams.

Embrace your worth, your light, your voice,
For in you resides the power of choice.
Stand tall, and let your dreams take flight,
For you are a beacon, shining so bright.

WHO IS NEXT?

Oh, the anguish, the uncertainty in your heart,
Who'll suffer next, in this tragic part?
In a world where innocence is too often betrayed,
Darkness encroaches, lives left dismayed.

The names of the fallen echo with despair,
Ochanya, Uwa, Sylvester, stories too hard to bear.
Now, Keren-Happuch, stands at the brink,
A victim of a society that fails to protect, to think.

Mother's regret, siblings' bewildered gaze,
They mourn the loss of your light, lost in a haze.
In a land where children's plight is ignored,
Darkness persists, hearts shattered and sore.

No child should bear such unspeakable pain,
No family should suffer loss again and again.
In this world of uncertainty and dread,
Who knows whose child's next to tread?

Together we must stand, united in this fight,
To shine a light on injustice, with all our might.
For every child deserves safety, love, respect,
To grow and flourish, free from neglect.

The stories of Ochanya, Sylvester, and you,
Must awaken the world, injustice to undo.
Let's work tirelessly, bring a brighter day,
Where no innocent lives are taken away.

The answer to your question rests in our hands,
To protect the vulnerable, take firm stands.
Striving for a world where all children are free,
From the darkness that threatens their destiny.

DEAFENING SILENCE

The deafening silence that surrounds you,
The lack of voices to speak for what is true.
It's a haunting reminder of the powerplay,
Where profit and self-interest dictate the way.

While you were silenced against your will,
Others choose silence for their own thrill.
They trade their conscience for fleeting credit
Leaving justice and truth to suffer a debit

From your grave, you long to be heard,
To have your story acknowledged, justice conferred.
But the principalities and powers turn a deaf ear,
Blinded by their own interests, consumed by fear.

Yet, in the collective voices raised at your death,
There lies a glimmer of hope, a flickering breath.
For in unity, we can break the chains of silence,
And demand accountability, exposing the violence.

Let us speak not for profit, but for what is right,
To shine a light on the darkness, to fight the fight.
Together, our voices can break the oppressive silence,
And ensure that justice prevails, breaking the defiance.

Though you were silenced, your words still resonate,
In the hearts and minds of those who won't hesitate.
To speak up, to stand tall, to demand a change,
To break the silence, and let truth rearrange.

May your plea for justice be heard and answered,
May your story inspire courage and awareness.
For in breaking the deafening silence, we find strength,
To build a world where justice and truth shall prevail at length.

TRUST

Trust, a leap of faith, vulnerability's embrace,
A gamble we take, it might be misplaced.
Should betrayal dictate our every move,
Or learn to trust with caution, our path to improve?

Though some may misuse trust, leaving wounds behind,
Others honour it, a beacon in darkness they find.
Trust can be a light, guiding us right,
Restoring our vision, dispelling the night.

So, trust with caution, discernment in your grasp,
Don't close off, nor let trust slip from your clasp.
In the balance between trust and caution's reign,
Navigate a world where trust can both heal and pain.

WHY ME?

In the vast expanse of existence, questions arise,
"Why me?" we ponder, tears in our eyes.
Among countless souls, why this chosen role?
To bear the darkness, endure the bitter toll.

It's a riddle, an enigma, answers elude,
Why some carry burdens, others in quietude.
In depths of despair, we seek explanations,
In life's ever-shifting, mysterious vibrations.

Yet, perhaps the answer lies not in who we are,
Nor in our flaws, or how we've journeyed far.
Sometimes, it's the whims of fate's turning wheel,
A cruel twist that wounds, making hearts steel.

But within the pain, strength can ascend,
Resilience born, refusing to bend.
In the throes of suffering's relentless chase,
Grows potential, finding grace's embrace.

So, while the question lingers, answers concealed,
Know you bear a power, an unconquerable shield.
Why you were chosen, you may never comprehend,
But through your journey, a story you'll extend.

In your pain, you may touch another's heart,
Bringing solace and healing, a brand-new start.
As you rise, let your strength inspire and be,
A testament to the human spirit's undying spree.

Amidst life's uncertainty, keep faith aflame,
In this world, your presence has purpose to claim.
Though questions may haunt, let resilience decree,
Forge ahead with courage, embrace what will be.

ECHOES OF STRIVE

In a land stained with blood, darkness prevails,
Carnivorous personalities, their evil trails.
A victim, like Uriah, caught in their strife,
Imperialism clashes with neo-imperialist life.

A state teeters on the edge, hanging in despair,
As fear grips the land, leaving us aware,
Peace eludes our grasp, slipping through our fingers,
In a nation consumed by conflict, anguish lingers.

First, Boko Haram emerged with its violent sway,
Spreading terror, seeking lives to slay.
Then came IPOB, adding to the fray,
Both driven by bloodlust, causing dismay.

Once known for its peace, a tranquil retreat,
Now a breeding ground for the deadliest feat.
These terror groups, hungry for bloodshed,
Unconcerned whose blood is freely shed.

In this land of turmoil, where chaos abounds,
We yearn for solace, for peace to resound.
May the voices of reason rise above the fray,
To guide us towards a brighter, peaceful day.

Let us unite against violence and strife,
Working together to rebuild our lives.
With hope in our hearts and resilience in our souls,
We can overcome the darkness, achieve our goals.

For blood may be spilled, but it does not define,
The spirit of a nation, the strength that's mine.
In the face of adversity, we shall stand tall,
Resisting the call of violence, embracing peace for all.

GAGGED

My mouth taped, and my hands tightly bound,
I am silenced, unable to make a sound.
The pain I endure, the violation I face,
Yet society expects me to embrace grace,
For stigma and shame have me gagged.

Raped and violated, a brutal assault,
The agony I bear, but my voice is stifled.
I'm told to keep it all inside,
My pain and suffering, I must hide,
For culture and tradition have me gagged.

Deprived of education, a commodity to be sold,
Traded off for marriage, my future foretold,
Silenced and confined to the fireside,
My dreams and aspirations pushed aside,
For society's expectations have me gagged.

But who will remove the tape, to free my voice?
Who will let me make a choice?
It is my quandary, my struggle to find,
As an African girl, who will unbind,
And ungag me from these chains?

Yet we seek to rise, with determination and might,
Facing the challenges, standing for what's right.
In the midst of fear and uncertainty,
We raise our voices, united in solidarity,
With our eyes to the skies, seeking signs of hope.

We may resign to chance, but we won't back down,
For together we fight, to reshape our town.
The jungle rumbles with our collective roar,
As we break free from the chains that bore,
And we strive to shape a brighter tomorrow.

THE AFRICAN GIRL

How else would you know
She's an African girl
If not for the tape across her mouth,
To drown her voice, diminishing her worth?

If not for the chains that bind her hands,
Restrict her from taking a stand.
Would you still see the strength within her?
Would you see resilience that stops her flight?

How else would you know
She's an African girl
If she fought back against violence,
Defying the norms with defiance?

If her tears flowed freely and unashamed,
If justice was not just a game.
Would you recognize the fire in her eyes,
The determination that never dies?

How else would you know
She's an African girl
If she demanded her rightful place,
And claimed her space with grace?

If she embraced her heritage and legacy,
And built a future that sets her free.
Would you acknowledge her worth,
The brilliance she brought to this Earth?

How else would you know
She's an African girl
If she pursued an education; her dreams,
Broke barriers, tore at the seams?

If her voice rang out, no longer suppressed,
If her rights were honoured, no longer repressed.
Would you see the possibilities she held,
The stories of triumph waiting to be told?

Now, who gags the gagger?
Who untapes her mouth and sets her free?
Who obliterates the stigma, the discrimination,
And creates a world of equal liberation?

It is a collective effort, a united stand,
To uplift every African girl in this land.
For they are strong, resilient, and bold,
They break barriers, shaping a future untold.

CIRCUMCISION

In the depths of tradition, it is believed
That through circumcision, a woman achieves
The path to womanhood, they proclaim,
But at what cost? What price to pay?

Forced into a dark and dingy hut,
Legs pried open; bodies held in a rut.
The clinking of instruments, a chilling sound,
As scissors, razors, and knives are found.

The pain is unbearable, the blood flows,
A river of suffering, a lifetime of woes.
Why this sacrifice, this cruel act?
To mold a woman's desires, to control her intact?

They say it is to prevent promiscuity,
To safeguard a woman's purity.
But tales are whispered, secrets unfold,
Of women robbed of pleasure, their spirits sold.

In the neighbouring village, a nympho's plight,
Her pleasure mound gone; her soul takes flight.
In the village nearby, a maiden's shame,
Bedwetting, a reminder of a lost flame.

Why dehumanise a woman, strip her of bliss,
Deny her the ecstasy of nature's kiss?
She deserves to embrace her own desire,
To experience pleasure, to light her fire.

Let us question these traditions old,
Challenge the beliefs that leave hearts cold.
Empower women with choices, voices strong,
Respect their bodies, where they belong.

For no woman should endure such pain,
Her dignity and pleasure should always remain.
Let us unite to break these chains,
And celebrate the beauty that womanhood contains.

STOLEN INNOCENCE

Within this sacred temple I reside,
Guarded fervently for God's grace to find,
But alas! A predator approached with dark intent,
To violate my sanctuary, innocence designed.

A wild creature masked among humanity's guise,
Unleashing fury like a tempest's wrath,
He defiled what I held dear, so sanctified,
Desecrating purity on an unholy path.

Once as pure as snow, now tainted scarlet red,
He crushed my innocence with his cruel desire,
Imposing guilt upon me, tears left unshed,
A victim silenced, consumed by inner fire

IN HIS IMAGE

From shared womb we both emerged, entwined
Nourished by one cord, our common lifeline
Yet destiny's scales tip unequally
You the favoured heir, while I'm unseen

You wear the crown, the head adorned with pride
I'm relegated to the tail or neck
While you explore the world with carefree stride
I'm tethered to the fireside, a speck

They say, "What's good for goose is good for gander"
But why am I deprived of pleasures known?
Discrimination's grasp, a hurtful slander
When in God's eyes, we're equally His own

In the sacred Book, we're called to be peers
Children of God, reflections of His grace
Made in His image, devoid of all fears
Together we shall rise, in love embrace

DILEMMA

They malign me in measures so unfair
Above reason, their words linger in the air
Denigrating my dignity with disdain
Deep-seated enmity, a hurtful campaign

Malice oozes like a never-ending spring
As a girl child in a society's sting
They silence my voice, deny me an opinion
Reducing me to a figurehead's dominion

A plaything, manipulated at their behest
They restrict my choices, their power manifest
Labeling me rebellious, disobedient
Yet all I seek is freedom, my rights apparent

For the right to choose is a sacred plea
To shape my own destiny, to set myself free
To embrace my dignity, unleash my talent
And fulfil my purpose with courage gallant

We are all born to find our own unique way
To walk our own paths, to seize the day
Let me choose, empower me to be strong
For destiny awaits, a journey lifelong

THE WALLS WE BUILD

Blinded by despise, they fail to see
The goodness that resides within our hearts
In chains of slavery, they hold the key
Suppressing voices, tearing us apart

Yet in their ignorance, they fail to grasp
That without us, they cannot truly soar
Their wives, behind the walls, a life unasked
Their voices muted, longing to explore

With the big stick, they silence any plea
Their daughters, sisters, mothers feel the pain
While in another home, hypocrisy
They serve oppression, their ego's gain

But why build walls to keep the sunlight out?
When unity and strength could light the way
Dismantle biases, erase the doubt
Embrace the talents women can display

For in the harmony of hearts and minds
Two heads united, wisdom's journey begun
With biases shattered, love entwined
Together we'll proclaim, "Two heads are one!"

IGNORANCE

Professors spew words of violence, so loud
Unlettered men in peace's plea
Muslims and Christians, faith in their shroud
Claiming peace, yet living in disharmony

They rise to fight, defending their God's name
Forgetting that He's mighty in His might
Victorious battles won through love's flame
His weapons: knowledge, love shining bright

If only they could grasp this truth profound
Rather than fight, seek to truly know Him
Delve deep into books, where answers are found
Discover His nature, love to the brim

For in the realm of love and knowledge pure
Resides the essence of the divine soul
If they could seek, strife would find no allure
And harmony would prevail as their goal

ENCHANTED

If I were an artist skilled and adept
I'd paint a masterpiece with tender care,
A picture of your beauty so adept,
In its raw essence, naked and so fair.

Each brushstroke capturing your wondrous grace,
Revealing curves and alluring symmetry,
Your vital statistics in perfect space,
A celebration of your womanly decree.

But alas, I am a poet, retired long,
Tragedies consumed my poetic flame,
My collection of verses lost in the throng,
Destroyed by fire, leaving naught but shame.

Yet your enchanting image, oh so divine,
Awakens my dormant hunger for verses,
So let me compare you to a summer's night,
But truly, your loveliness shines bright.

THE TEMPLE

In distant lands, an island unknown,
Where mortals' feet have never trod,
There, my love, I'd take thee alone,
To fashion thee a temple of the gods.

In sacred rites, we'd both partake,
As ardent worshipper and divine,
Your pleasure, my devotion, inextricably awake,
An offering of joy, endlessly entwined.

Within those hallowed walls we'd dwell,
Indulging in passion's sacred art,
Your moans, like hymns, their stories tell,
As love's symphony enthrals the heart.

In this temple of love, we'd find our place,
In your acceptance, my soul's release,
Bound by desire's unyielding embrace,
Together, in bliss, our love would increase.

SHAME

In the break of dawn, shadows veil the sky,
A weighty dusk that obscures our way,
Fearful of stumbling, we dare not fly,
Holding onto hope, clinging to a tusk's sway.

Silent steps we take, words left unsaid,
Fearful of the arrows that truth may hurl,
We wander, lost, from pillar to thread,
Avoiding the piercing point, our spirits unfurl.

Heads bowed low, burdened by shame,
Aching hearts and souls filled with pain,
Our courage wanes, our will to reclaim,
A chain of bleeding wounds, a cruel refrain.

Yet we feast and revel, like fish in a sea,
Indulging in excess, like swine in their sty,
Drinking the poison, embracing duplicity,
Our foolishness our crime, our senses awry.

Yearning for change, yet dreading its might,
A daunting path we tread, uncertain ground,
Craving the crown, earned through righteous fight,
In our pursuit, we sacrifice truth, lost and drowned.

A PRAYER

In this life's hive of strife and strain,
We hold onto the bond we attain,
Pitching high to sail above the fray,
Clawing through thorns as we find our way.

With fiery breath, desire ignites,
We chase our dreams with all our might,
Heads held high, lips sighing in bliss,
As life's currents guide us with a kiss.

In moments of joy, sadness may ensue,
Yet I trust in You to lift me anew,
To calm my fears and ease my doubt,
As Your divine presence carries me out.

So, I pray, Oh Lord, with all my heart,
Grant me strength, let Your love impart,
Guide me on this journey I tread,
With Your grace, I shall be led.

A MESSAGE TO HEAVEN

On this day of mixed emotions,
A bittersweet wave of commotions,
I wear a long face, it's true,
For my heart's burden, only I knew.

While others cheer for my new phase,
I dwell in sorrow, lost in a daze,
The gloom surrounds me like a shroud,
As I mourn silently, not too loud.

Many my age have departed,
Life's cruel hand has swiftly charted,
Their paths to realms beyond our sight,
Leaving us behind in the fading light.

So, questions come like pouring rain,
Why not rejoice, why bear this pain?
I should celebrate life's grand display,
But my birthday marks her death day.

The gift of life, I'm blessed to possess,
Yet, her absence leaves my soul in distress,
For every year, on this special date,
I remember her, my dear one's fate.

In the midst of joy and cake's delight,
I'll light a candle for her in the night,
Remembering the love, we once shared,
In my heart, her memory's ensnared.

A sad day it may be, this is true,
But her presence in my heart, she grew,
And as I blow out the candles' blaze,
I'll send a message to her, in heaven's maze.

A LOVE STORY

Amidst the doubts and sceptic's gaze,
We stood together, unfazed,
For they questioned our endeavour,
Claiming resources, we would sever.

But we, undeterred, held hands tight,
Knowing love's wealth would be our light,
For riches aren't measured in gold,
But in the love our hearts unfold.

With confidence in our bond's embrace,
We walked our path with grace,
For love was our foundation strong,
And faith in each other, where we belong.

Against the odds, we ventured on,
Wings of faith, our spirits drawn,
Propelled by the power of our love,
A force that soared on wings above.

With love as our compass, we found our way,
Creating peace and progress day by day,
For where love resides, miracles unfold,
And harmony becomes the tale we mold.

So, let them wonder and question still,
As our love story we continue to fulfil,
For the resources we truly possess,
Are love, trust, and happiness.

BEYOND THE BLUE SKY

In realms beyond the vast blue sky,
Where new horizons catch the eye,
Above the earthly plane we soar,
A crop of hope, forevermore.

Seeking justice for the pain,
The depths of evil we disdain,
I see you, pensive, filled with sorrow,
In search of answers for tomorrow.

If I could reach you, oh, my dear,
And wipe away each falling tear,
Know that I've found a new abode,
In radiant white, a joyful ode.

In the realm of white clouds I reside,
A haven where love and peace collide,
My home, so bright, a heavenly glow,
Where I embrace a life aglow.

Though I'm absent from your sight,
In the celestial realm of light,
Take solace in knowing, my dear friend,
Our connection shall never end.

For in the white clouds, high above,
Our bond transcends, eternal love,
And as you journey here on Earth,
Remember our souls share a sacred worth.

DIAMOND IN THE ROUGH

In the depths of her despair,
Toyin Falaye, burdened by the weight she'd bear,
Emotionally abused, assaulted, and torn,
Her self-worth shattered; her spirit worn.

From childhood's grasp, she felt unworthy,
Each experience chipping away, hurting deeply.
Verbal daggers pierced her fragile esteem,
Leaving scars unseen, a haunting dream.

Depression gripped her, a captor so cruel,
Suicide's allure, an obsession to duel,
Yet, death itself hesitated, its fangs withdrawn,
For her purpose remained, her light not gone.

Her attempts thwarted, life's calling unmet,
Restlessness consumed her, causing a fret.
But amidst the darkness, a glimmer appeared,
The light of God, dispelling her fear.

Guiding her path, igniting her soul,
Toyin found purpose, her purpose to console,
To help fellow victims rise above their strife,
Transforming their stories, embracing new life.

A beacon of hope, she stands strong and tall,
Liberating others, answering their call,
Turning pain to glory, wounds to wisdom's gain,
Toyin Falaiye, a testament of resilience and renewal.

THE WALL

Why forsake love's beauty, its wondrous allure,
Because a hurtful encounter made your heart endure?
Why forsake the butterfly's pure delight,
Their magical presence, casting hues so bright?

Love is a victor, though it may bring defeat,
For in its depths, both pain and joy entreat.
Thus, as you construct a shield from the ache,
You bar love's rewards in your wake.

Therefore, tread with an open heart and soul,
Embrace the journey - the high and the low.
As the wall crumble for love's gifts to unfold
Unveiling the beauty for you to behold.

TWICE A VICTIM

In a society where justice is amiss,
And victims of abuse are dismissed,
She finds the courage to seek aid,
To report the crime, unafraid.

"Inspector, please, I implore,
He violated me to my core.
Now, my life's in jeopardy,
For speaking out against my enemy.

“Please, protect me, save my soul."
But the response leaves her heart cold.
"Why did you go to his place?
Why can't you stay in one space?

Look at the clothes you wear,
No wonder he couldn't resist the snare.
Why would he exercise control?
You brought it upon yourself, they'll extol."

She now understands the bitter truth,
Why her friends warned, her heart uncouth,
In this society, the victim's blamed,
Shamed and humiliated, their worth maimed.

Even when the police lend an ear,
Their motive is tainted; their intentions clear.
For monetary gains, they seek compromise,
Between the rapist and victim's cries.

In that exchange, a commission lies,
As justice withers, their empathy dies.
Twice a victim, she's left to bear,
The weight of injustice, the burden unfair.

But she won't be silenced, she won't retreat,
She'll fight for justice, to make the truth complete.
For every voice that's raised, for every soul,
She'll stand in solidarity, to reclaim control.

I WISH I KNEW

Oh, the painful lesson learned,
In a world where knowledge turned.
They promised education's might,
But concealed the darkness from sight.

To know the power of the pen,
Should never mean harm to women.
If only the truth had been revealed,
The wounds and scars could have been healed.

I share your wish, dear soul,
That you had known and taken control.
But let us forge a path anew,
Where education empowers, and truth shines through.

May your voice now rise strong and clear,
To educate others, dispelling the fear.
Together, we'll strive for a world that's just,
Where education empowers and respects all of us.

BREAKING THE CHAINS

In the shadows, they conceal their sin,
Faking righteous anger to hide within.
But their conscience knows the weight,
Of lies they've woven, small and great.

Each untruth whispered, dark and cold,
A tangled web, their story unfolds.
Their fear of truth keeps them confined,
A never-ending cycle, it reminds.

Yet, truth cannot forever be denied,
It yearns for freedom, to be untied.
Their facade of virtue, paper-thin,
Will crumble when truth's light shines in.

Let us grope for truth's embrace,
For only then can we find grace.
Release the chains of falsehood's hold,
With righteous honesty, be bold.

UNBOWED

Amidst their attempts to break my will,
To silence my voice, to instil fear and chill,
I stood unbowed, resolute in my quest,
For justice and truth, I'd give my best.

They sent their forces, threats in disguise,
But I refused to yield, to compromise.
Their friends and allies, tried me to sway,
But I remained steadfast, come what may.

I granted them audience, played their game
But saw through their motives, felt their shame.
They defended their interests, not the truth,
Their actions, I found repulsive and uncouth.

And as I raised my voice, demanding justice,
Pressuring the government to awaken from its slumber,
They served me a love letter, threatening to sue,
But I stood my ground, knowing I'd done no wrong.

They sued me, hoping to silence my cries,
To intimidate and stifle, with legal ties.
But I refused to be silenced, for how could I be,
When the innocent blood of a child cried out to me?

I remained unwavering, undeterred in my plight,
For justice must prevail, in the face of their might.
I stood for truth, for the voiceless and oppressed,
Unbowed, until my cry for justice is addressed.

SILENT TEARS

Someday, from the depths of the grave,
My tears shall break the silence
They will speak of the unspeakable pain,
The horrors endured, my suffering in vain.

Someday, my tears shall provide the answers,
To the questions asked by countless in clusters.
They will reveal the truth, unmask the lies,
Expose the darkness hidden behind their disguise.

Someday, my tears shall compel the guilty,
To confess their sins, admit to their debauchery.
They will be held accountable for their deeds,
No longer hiding behind power and misdeeds.

Believe, for justice will not be denied,
Someday, the truth will no longer hide.
The abuser and those who shielded his name,
Will face the consequences, bear the blame.

It is only a matter of time, have faith,
The tears from the grave will pave the way.
For justice to prevail, for healing to begin,
Someday, the light of truth will shine from within.

HE TOOK EVERYTHING

He took everything she had,
Her money, her dreams, her jòy so sad.
He controlled her life, her every move,
Leaving her bruised, with nothing to prove.

She accepted his control, against her will,
Thinking it was normal, accepting the chill.
He painted her face with violence and pain,
Leaving her broken in tearful disdain.

She held on, hoping for change to come,
Afraid to leave, fearing what would be done.
But he grew worse, his darkness prevailed,
Until one fateful day, her life he drained.

He took her life, cutting it short and cruel,
And suddenly, those who knew her began to fuel
Their voices, sharing her story of abuse,
Realising too late the depth of her misuse.

But it was too late, for she was gone,
Her life extinguished, her spirit withdrawn.
Their words, though true, could not bring her back,
They were left with guilt, for the courage they lacked.

Her tale of abuse, silenced for so long,
Echoed now, a tragic and haunting song.
But in the aftermath, let us remember her name,
And vow to fight against abuse and its deadly flame.

BREAK THE CYCLE

Dare to be different.
You vowed to never become like him,
To reject violence and instead embrace empathy and compassion.
You have the power to break the cycle,
To be different, to create a new legacy.

Dare to be different.
In a world that often glorifies aggression,
Choose kindness and understanding as your weapons.
Speak up against injustice, but with respect and grace,
And let your words carry the weight of truth, not fists.

Dare to be different.
Remember the pain you witnessed,
The fear that gripped your heart,
And use it as a reminder of the harm caused by violence.
Be a beacon of hope in a world that desperately needs it.

Darc to be different.
You have the ability to rewrite your story,
To heal the wounds of the past and build a future of peace.
Break free from the chains of your father's actions,
And forge a path that reflects the goodness within you.

Dare to be different.
By inspiring others to do the same.
Choose love over hate,
And let your actions speak volumes,
For through compassion true change is made.

OCHANYA

In the depths of darkness, a tale unfolds,
Of a father and son, whose hearts turned cold.
The fraternal duo, a sinister pair,
Who shattered innocence without a care.

Ochanya, so young, her spirit bright,
Entrusted to their care, a fateful night.
But behind closed doors, a sinister game,
A twisted secret, causing endless shame.

For five long years, they took their turns,
Their monstrous acts, a fire that burns.
Innocence stolen, a childhood lost,
As their cruelty exerted a heavy cost.

Oh, Andrew and Victor, your actions so vile,
A betrayal of trust, a heart-wrenching trial.
How could you succumb to such wicked desire,
Inflicting pain on a soul so tender, so dire?

You thought you'd escape, without consequence,
But the truth prevails, it leaves no pretence.
Your names shall forever be etched in disdain,
As we raise our voices, our anger we sustain.

What a traitor you are as a father,
Your duty was to nurture a child with care
But you opted to torture her with horror rather
Plunging her into the abyss of pain and despair.

And you her fleeing cousin shall forever be known,
As one who sowed darkness and doom.
Your actions have thrown a family into endless gloom
Leaving scars and sorrow, an everlasting flame.

May your guilt weigh heavy upon your souls,
As the world condemns your wicked roles.
Ochanya's spirit shall rise above the pain,
As we fight for justice, her voice shall remain.

For every survivor, we'll stand up tall,
Their stories, their strength, we'll heed the call.
To bring an end to this cycle of abuse,
To protect the vulnerable, to let truth diffuse.

May Ochanya's light shine on forever,
As a symbol of courage, a stinging reminder
The chains that bind, the darkness that lingers,
In our pursuit of justice, our resolve never withers.

Oh, you paedophiles, may your guilt be profound,
As the weight of your sins comes crashing down.
May your names forever be stained by shame,
For the heinous acts that put out Ochanya's light.

BEYOND OUTRAGE

Beyond outrage, a chorus arises,
Voices united, demanding no compromises.
They rally in droves, for justice they fight,
In the face of darkness, a beacon of light.

But government's silence falls like a shroud,
Leaving the family alone in the crowd.
With treachery lurking, their burden grows,
Yet they remain steadfast, resilience shows.

Carrying their cross, heavy and immense,
Driven by conviction, fueled by defense.
For her memory, they forge ahead,
Determined to ensure no more tears are shed.

In their quest for justice, they stand tall,
Knowing her death shall not be in vain at all.
Their battle, a testament to love and care,
To end child sexual abuse, a burden to bear.

Though the road is long, filled with strife,
Their unwavering spirit gives them life.
With every step taken, they pave the way,
For a future where innocence will have its say.

AN ELEGY FOR OCHANYA

In solemn words and heartfelt lament,
We gather here, our voices spent,
To honour a soul whose light was dimmed,
Ochanya Elizabeth forever within.

Oh, beloved Ochanya, innocent and pure,
Your life cut short, our hearts endure,
A victim of cruelty, of heinous sin,
A battle you fought, but couldn't win.

A tender flower, in bloom so bright,
Snatched away in the darkest night,
Your spirit touched us with grace untold,
As stories of your pain began to unfold.

In the depths of injustice, your voice arose,
A cry for change, for those who oppose,
A world where children are safe from harm,
Where their dreams can flourish, free from alarm.

We mourn your loss, with heavy hearts,
For the innocence stolen, torn apart,
But we'll carry your memory, like a torch,
A beacon of hope, never to scorch.

Oh! Ochanya! We pledge to fight,
For justice and truth, with all our might,
To ensure no more souls suffer your fate,
In a world where love should conquer hate.

Your name shall be etched upon our souls,
A reminder of the battle that unfolds,
To protect the vulnerable, to heal the pain,
In your memory, our efforts shall remain.

Rest now, dear Ochanya, in eternal peace,
May your spirit find solace, may it find release,
Though your time was short, your impact profound,
In our hearts, your presence forever will resound.

Farewell, sweet soul, may you find your rest,
In the arms of love, forever blessed,
Your legacy lives on, in the fight we wage,
To bring an end to the darkness of this age.

In honor of Elizabeth, our voices rise,
Demanding justice, no compromise,
For every child whose innocence is torn,
May a new era be born.

WE ARE ALL KEREN-HAPPUCH

We are all Keren-Happuch, in heart and in soul,
Bound together by a shared pain, an unbearable toll.
Through her story, we see the reflection of our own,
The countless voices silenced, the anguish unknown.

In the depths of her sorrow, we find our own grief,
For the violence endured, causing souls to seethe.
We carry her burden, her pain we embrace,
For in her tragedy, we see change to take place.

We are all Keren-Happuch, united as one,
In the fight against injustice, the battle not yet won.
Her spirit lives on, igniting a fire within,
To stand up, to speak out, until justice we win.

In her memory, we rise with might,
Demanding accountability, for every wrong we'll fight.
No longer silent, our voices shall resound,
In solidarity, we create a world profound.

We are all Keren-Happuch, survivors of the storm,
Carrying the scars, but refusing to conform.
We reclaim our power, reclaim our worth,
For in unity and resilience, we find our rebirth.

Together, we rise, unstoppable and strong,
Breaking the chains that have silenced us for long.
No longer victims, but warriors of light,
We stand tall, we rise, with all our might.

We are all Keren-Happuch, a beacon of hope,
A testament to resilience, the strength to cope.
In her name, we pledge to break the cycle of pain,
To create a world where justice and healing reign.

So, let us stand together, hand in hand,
United in purpose, a formidable band.
For we are all Keren-Happuch, forever intertwined,
In the pursuit of justice, our hearts aligned.

MY PLEDGE

I pledge, as a voice for the voiceless,
I stand, Lemmy Ughegbe, a resolute hand,
To seek justice, unwavering and true,
For Keren-Happuch and all who've suffered too.

In the face of darkness, I will not yield,
For the wounds inflicted, I'll never shield.
With every breath, my resolve takes flight,
To bring forth justice, shining a relentless light.

For Keren-Happuch, a symbol of pain,
Her spirit whispers, urging me to sustain.
I'll champion her cause, her story I'll tell,
With unwavering determination, unyielding in this swell.

To every victim, survivor, unheard,
Your pain and your stories will not be blurred.
I'll fight for your rights, your voices I'll raise,
In the pursuit of justice, through all the dismays.

I'll navigate the hurdles, the challenges that lie,
With persistence, compassion, I'll amplify,
The cries for justice, the call for change,
In a system where equality must rearrange.

In Nigeria's tapestry, I'll weave a new thread,
Where justice is served, where hope is widespread.
With resilience as my armour, courage as my guide,
I'll stand by your side, never stepping aside.

I pledge to be unyielding, in this noble quest,
To build a safer world, where all are blessed.
No victim, no survivor, shall be left behind,
As we strive for justice, a new era to find.

For Keren-Happuch and every wounded soul,
Your stories fuel my fire, they make me whole.
Together we'll walk, in unity and grace,
Seeking justice for each heart that's misplaced.

I pledge to remain untiring, my spirit unbound,
In the pursuit of justice, where solace is found.
For Keren-Happuch, for every victim and survivor,
In this battle for justice, I am an unwavering driver.

And so, I raise my voice, in solidarity and might,
To seek justice, to make things right.
With unwavering determination, I'll fight the fight,
For Keren-Happuch, others and for what is right.

WHERE IS THY HONOUR?

Oh, lawmakers, who seek to be called "honourables,"
Yet lack the honour to fulfil your own fables.
You passed a resolution, so grand and bold,
To probe the tragedy that's left our hearts cold.

But here we stand, years have passed by,
Since that fateful day, the resolution in the sky.
You wear your titles with pomp and pride,
But where is the honour you claim to abide?

A 14-year-old girl-child, her innocence shattered,
Raped and slained, her dreams forever scattered.
You made promises, words so empty and hollow,
While her memory fades, lost in the sorrow.

We are honourables," you say, with a cynical smile,
But where is the honour in your guile?
You sit in your chambers, so comfortable and high,
While justice for Keren-Happuch is left to die.

You seek accolades, praise, and respect,
But what about the duty you must protect?
To serve the people, to hold truth dear,
Instead, you turn a blind eye, perpetuating fear.

Oh, lawmakers, the irony is stark and clear,
To call yourselves "honourables" is insincere.
For true honour lies in actions, not just in name,
And justice delayed is justice maimed.

You may forget, but we will remember,
The girl whose life was stolen, her soul in ember.
Your inaction speaks volumes, louder than words,
Leaving a bitter taste, like the sting of betrayal.

So, go on, "honourable," in your charade,
But know that your dishonour is forever engraved.
For when the time comes, and judgment is due,
Your lack of honour will be exposed, that much is true.

The memory of Keren-Happuch will not fade away,
A reminder of the justice you failed to convey.
Your titles mean nothing, if honour is not earned,
For true honour is a flame that cannot be burned.

JEOPARDY

In a world where justice should prevail,
We stand appalled, our hearts deeply impaled.
Keren-Happuch, a name forever etched,
In the annals of a system that failed to protect.

Fourteen years young, her life cut short,
A victim of heinous acts, a pain hard to distort.
Yet the police, entrusted with the pursuit of right,
Turned a blind eye, shrouded in apathy's night.

Government agencies, their duty to uphold,
Justice denied, as stories remain untold.
Keren-Happuch's cries echo in the wind,
As those in power let justice rescind.

The pillars of law, crumble with disgrace,
Leaving scars that time alone can't erase.
In the face of injustice, we raise our voice,
Demanding accountability, a rightful choice.

For every Keren-Happuch, we will not rest,
Until her story is heard, justice manifest.
No longer will we tolerate their negligence,
Their indifference, a stain on our conscience.

To the police and government agencies, we say,
You failed Keren-Happuch in the gravest ways.
But we'll persist, unyielding in our fight,
For a system that safeguards, that sets things right.

Let this be a call to mend what's broken,
To ensure no more lives are forsaken.
Hold the guilty accountable, let truth prevail,
And in Keren-Happuch's name, let justice sail.

We stand in solidarity, her memory we cherish,
Her spirit emboldening us, our resolve will not perish.
For every silenced victim, we'll continue to demand,
That the police and government finally take a stand.

In the face of adversity, we'll rise together,
A united voice, a force that cannot be severed.
Until justice is served, until the truth is revealed,
For Keren-Happuch and others, we'll forever wield.

May her soul find solace, in the arms of peace,
As we fight for justice, until it's finally released.
In the pursuit of truth, we'll relentlessly strive,
For Keren-Happuch, may her spirit forever survive.

CITADELS OF LEARNING

In halls of learning, where knowledge should abide,
A disheartening truth, we can no longer deny.
Schools once noble, now driven by greed,
As they prioritise profits over the students' need.

In pursuit of wealth, they lose sight,
Of their sacred duty, to nurture the light.
For education's essence goes beyond a price,
It's about shaping minds, igniting their rise.

But behold the institutions, where money rules all,
Where students are commodities, ready to enthral.
The welfare of children cast aside in the race,
As their well-being becomes a mere footnote to chase.

Books are outdated, resources run dry,
Teachers overwhelmed, but who will ask why?
In this money-making game, the students suffer,
Their dreams diminished, their spirits buffer.

The focus shifts to numbers, to marketing schemes,
While nurturing potential becomes a pipe dream.
Policies bend, principles compromise,
As the value of education starts to capsize.

But we must raise our voices, challenge this trend,
For the future of our children, we must defend.
Education should be a sanctuary, a nurturing ground,
Where passion and growth are beautifully found.

Let us demand change, a shift in the tide,
Where students are cherished, their needs dignified.
Schools must remember their purpose, their core,
To mold young minds, inspiring forevermore.

For it is not just about the profits amassed,
But the lives transformed, as knowledge is amassed.
A plea to those in power, let compassion prevail,
To put students first, before the monetary trail.

Let education be a beacon of hope,
Where students are valued, their dreams elope.
May schools remember their sacred mission,
To shape young lives with love and compassion.

For in the end, it's not about monetary gain,
But the legacy we leave, the impact we retain.
Let us reclaim education's true worth,
For the sake of our children, their futures' rebirth.

GRIEF

In this time of anguish and deepest sorrow,
I offer my words, hoping to borrow,
A sliver of solace, a gentle embrace,
For a grieving mother, in this sacred space.

With heavy heart, I cannot fathom your pain,
The loss of a daughter, so young slained.
Words may fall short, but let my presence be,
A beacon of support that you see.

In this moment of darkness, I stand by your side,
To offer comfort as your tears freely glide.
The weight of the world feels so immense,
But know you're not alone, we share in your grief.

Your daughter, a precious soul, unfairly taken,
Her light extinguished; innocence forsaken.
In this unjust world, we find no reprieve,
But in your love, her spirit will forever live.

Though words cannot heal, they offer a thread,
To weave through the wounds that lay spread.
In memories cherished, her essence will dwell,
A guiding light, as you bid her farewell.

Take solace in knowing she was truly loved,
A beacon of joy, now watching from above.
Embrace the love that surrounds you, so true,

In each tender moment, she'll be there too.

Find strength in your tears, let them freely flow,
For grief is a river that helps us to grow.
In the depths of your pain, may resilience rise,
As you honour her spirit, and hear her cries.

May time be gentle, as you navigate,
The path of healing, amidst this heavy weight.
And know that love, in its infinite form,
Will guide you through this darkest storm.

Lean on the support of those who care,
As you traverse a world so unfair.
You are not alone in this sorrowful strife,
For together, we'll shine the torch on her life.

FOR SYLVESTER OROMONI JNR

In the halls of learning, where dreams should thrive,
A tragedy unfolded, cutting life's fragile ties.
Sylvester Oromoni Jnr, a bright young soul,
Innocence stolen, an unforgivable toll.

At tender twelve, with hopes held high,
His spirit pure, reaching for the sky.
But within those walls, a nightmare grew,
Where bullying shadows, heartlessly slew.

Senior students, wielding power and might,
Inflicted torment, casting away the light.
Forced to drink a toxic, cruel potion,
Sylvester's life tainted by this dark notion.

Oh, precious child, taken away too soon,
Injustice unleashed, staining our moon.
Your laughter silenced, a void in our hearts,
As we mourn the loss, the pain imparts.

We weep for your dreams, forever unrealised,
For the love extinguished, cruelly demised.
No words can express the depth of our sorrow,
For the loss of a soul, a bright tomorrow.

In this tragedy, we stand united and strong,
Demanding justice, ensuring the wrongs are long gone.
For every child, their safety we'll defend,
To ensure their innocence, we'll fiercely contend.

Sylvester Oromoni Jnr, your memory lives on,
A symbol of resilience, though your light is gone.
In our hearts, your spirit forever abides,
As we strive to protect the ones by your side.

Let us learn from this pain, let it serve as a call,
To create a world where kindness stands tall.
No child should suffer, their spirits confined,
May Sylvester's legacy forever us remind.

In the face of darkness, we'll kindle a light,
For Sylvester and others, who faced this cruel plight.
Together we'll strive, their voices to uplift,
To eradicate bullying, and create a healing shift.

ELEGY TO OSINACHI NWACHUKWU

In the realm of gospel, her voice did soar,
Osinachi Nwachukwu, an artist to adore.
A beacon of faith, her songs touched our souls,
But behind the scenes, a secret she holds.

Beneath the spotlight's warm and loving glow,
A darkness lurked, where bruises did grow.
Victim of domestic violence's cruel hand,
Her spirit tested, her strength tried and banned.

With grace she sang, her voice piercing through,
Yet the pain she bore, only a chosen few knew.
Behind closed doors, where fear consumed,
Her talents blossomed, but her heart was doomed.

In each note she sang, a prayer did reside,
A plea for freedom, to break free from the tide.
Her music became a sanctuary of hope,
A refuge for healing, helping her to cope.

But today we gather with heavy hearts,
To mourn the loss of her vibrant arts.
For the violence she faced, silenced her voice,
Leaving us here, to grieve her choice.

Osinachi Nwachukwu, we honour your strength,
In the face of adversity, you persevered at length.
Your talents remain, forever enshrined,
In the hearts of those you left behind.

We pledge to carry your legacy with pride,
To speak against violence, to stand side by side.
In the gospel realm, your spirit lives on,
A testament to faith, unyielding and strong.

May your soul find solace in eternal peace,
As your melodies in our hearts never cease.
We'll remember your gift, your spirit unbound,
As we pray for healing profound.

Though darkness may have marred your earthly flight,
Your voice continues to shine, forever bright.
Osinachi Nwachukwu, may you find release,
In the arms of grace, where pain finds its peace.

TEARS FOR KEREN

In solemn grace, we gather here today,
To honour a life lost along the way.
Keren-Happuch, a name forever imprinted,
In our hearts, a memory that's undiminished.

At fourteen, a tender bloom, full of dreams,
Her spirit radiant, or so it seems.
But darkness fell upon her innocent soul,
A cruel act of violence that took its toll.

In a world where safety should be assured,
She faced a horror no one should endure.
Her voice silenced, her spirit broken,
Yet her story must be spoken.

Keren-Happuch, we hear your silent cries,
We see the tears that stain our saddened skies.
Though your light was extinguished far too soon,
Your memory echoes, a mournful tune.

We mourn the loss of your unfulfilled years,
Of dreams untangled and hopes held dear.
The promise of tomorrow, snatched away,
Leaving us here, searching for words to say.

Injustice, like a tempest, rages on,
Yet your tragic fate cannot be undone.
But we vow, in your name, to take a stand,
To create a world where safety is at hand.

We'll speak out against the violence that scars,
Shattering the silence that hides the stars.
For you, dear Keren-Happuch, we'll persist,
Till justice is served, till darkness desists.

May your soul find solace in heavenly embrace,
As we gather strength to carry on your grace.
You'll forever remain in our hearts
A symbol of resilience and bravery.

Rest in peace, dear Keren-Happuch, so young,
Your memory, like a gentle song, will be sung.
In our quest for justice, your spirit will guide,
As we stand together, side by side

VICTIMS

In shadows deep, where anguish lies,
We gather here, with tearful eyes
In heartfelt words, we find our voice,
To honour victims, make a choice.

To those who've suffered, we proclaim,
Your pain, we see, we share your name.
In hearts burdened, scars concealed,
Your stories brave, now to be revealed.

In a world unkind, where darkness falls,
You've faced the depths, endured it all.
Your spirit shines, resilient and strong,
Though silenced, your courage sings its song.

For every soul touched by vile assault,
Our empathy, a blanket to exalt.
We stand united, resolute and firm,
Injustice challenged; we yearn to affirm.

To the survivors, we extend our care,
A sanctuary of love, we're here to share.
Your worth immeasurable, your light divine,
Together we heal, hearts intertwine.

Let empathy guide our collective way,
To dismantle systems that led astray.
With love as armour, we'll rise above,
Creating a world where justice and peace converge.

No more shall silence shroud their plea,
We vow to listen, to set them free.
With empathy, we break each chain,
To restore their dignity, to ease their pain.

May healing waters wash away their fears,
Replace anguish with hope that perseveres.
For they are warriors, resilient and bold,
With love and support, their stories unfold.

In this ode to victims, we make a stand,
To create a safer land.
Together we fight, until justice prevails,
For those who've suffered, our compassion avails.

A VICTIM'S TESTIMONY

In the realm of justice, a tale of despair unfolds,
Ochanya's words, a poignant testimony of truth told
Father and son, architects of her plight
Stealing her innocence, plunging into her with might

Her pleas, a symphony, unheard by her kin
Paying a deaf ear to the darkness within
Four years of trial, justice seemingly near
Yet in the end, the verdict we fear

In the courtroom, her words echo in the air,
A dying declaration, a plea for justice fair
But Justice Ityoyiman's decision, a fable untold,
Acquittal handed down her abusers; a story so cold

Video evidence speaks louder than the grave,
Yet the judge turns away, justice, to deprave
Ochanya's torment, a stain that won't fade,
In the ream of justice, a victim betrayed

MASQUERADE

Masquerades they are, season after season,
Descending from their high horses with false reason.
Donning garbs of deception, their true selves concealed,
Feigning humility while their motives are revealed.

Arrogance replaced with phantom empathy's guise,
As they seek tickets to the fortress that we despise.
Our hard-earned taxes built their sheltered abode,
Shielding them from the realities of our humble abode.

Season after season, they spin their web of lies,
Promising milk and honey while impoverishing our lives.
Yet we fall for their tricks, again and again,
Granting them the tickets for an extended reign.

How long shall we dance this unpleasant tune?
Are we charmed or blinded, caught in a gloomy swoon?
Why do we yield to their selfish desires and schemes,
When all they leave us with are empty dreams?

Season after season, they repeat the same refrain,
More promises, more illusions, nothing to sustain.
Mirages they present, illusions in the air,
Leaving us with naught but despair.

Now another season dawns, they approach once more,
Descending from their high horses to even the score.
They partake in our water, our humblest fare,
But their intentions remain sly and unfair.

But season after season, we've learned their game,
Refusing to be fooled, we rise to reclaim.
Determined for change, no longer deceived,
By those who sow harvests while we're left bereaved.

We won't be swayed by their empty charade,
While hunger and poverty cast their somber shade.
The time has come for us to break free,
From the masquerades, their deceptive decree.

For we hold the power to reshape our fate,
To stand united and forge a different state.
No more seasons of false promises and disguise,
We'll break the chains and see truth rise

MADNESS

The poet's madness, a unique realm untamed,
Not the madness of the streets, wild and unrestrained.
But akin to a pregnant woman's labour room,
For the poet carries ideas, waiting to bloom.

Like waves crashing upon a broken boat,
Ideas gather, fragments of a creative float.
Yet they remain unborn, their time not due,
A poetic madness, a birth yet to pursue.

Within the poet's mind, a chaotic storm brews,
A tempest of thoughts, swirling hues.
The canvas of words, a pregnant tapestry,
Yearning to birth verse, in poetic ecstasy.

But time lingers, and the ideas remain concealed,
The poet's madness, an ongoing ordeal.
The weight of unspoken words, a heavy burden,
Yet the poet perseveres, his passion unwavering'.

In the poet's madness, lies a world untold,
Whispered secrets waiting to unfold.
For within the chaos, beauty seeks its way,
A poetic birth, where words come to play.

So, embrace the poet's madness, unique and rare,
A glimpse into a realm beyond compare.
For within the pregnant mind of the poet,
Lies the magic of words, waiting to be set.

AUTHENTIC

In a world of pretences and masks we wear,
Our relationship stands out, bold and rare.
They label it problematic, unable to see,
The authenticity that binds you and me.

In a realm of make-believe and illusion,
We embrace the rawness, the truth's intrusion.
For it is through our quarrels and strife,
That we forge a bond, unbreakable for life.

They seek perfection, a flawless display,
But it's in our imperfections, we find our way.
Through disagreements and heated debates,
We navigate the storm, building stronger traits.

Our love is not a fairy tale, picture-perfect art,
But a canvas of realness, a reflection of our heart.
In our arguments, we find lessons to learn,
Growth and understanding, at every turn.

So let them label our relationship as they may,
For we know the truth that lights our way.
Authenticity we cherish, in each moment we share,
In the messiness of life, our love remains rare.

HOPE OF HAVEN

In the depths of fear and despair,
Yearning for a safe haven, so rare.
If only I could shield my mother's pain,
Protect my brothers from the abuser's reign.

A place where we could find refuge and peace,
Away from the horrors that refuse to cease.
A sanctuary where our voices could be heard,
To break the silence, speak the unspeakable word.

For countless souls trapped in the same plight,
Yearning for safety, longing for respite.
If they had a haven, free from the abuser's grip,
They would rise together, their voices equipped.

With courage in their hearts, they would proclaim,
The truth of their suffering, the weight of their shame.
Demanding justice for the innocence stolen,
Seeking retribution for the wounds that were woven.

But still, we search for that sacred ground,
Where the wounded souls can truly be found.
A safe haven that welcomes and protects,
Where survivors can heal, and pain disconnects.

Let us strive to create that sanctuary,
Where victims can find solace, finally be free.
For in unity and compassion, we can ignite,
A world where safety prevails, where darkness takes flight.

May every survivor find solace and light,
In a safe haven, where they can reclaim their might.
And together, let us stand against the abuser's hand,
Demanding justice, a world where all can safely stand.

SAFE HAVEN

In a world devoid of empathy's grace,
Where victims are silenced, their voices erased,
We yearn for a safe haven, a sanctuary true,
Where healing can begin, where hope can renew.

If I had known such a place to hide,
To shield my loved ones from pain's cruel tide,
I would have broken the silence, found my voice,
Protected them from the abuser's choice.

But countless others suffer in silence's grip,
Their voices stifled; their pain kept hidden deep.
If only they could find a haven secure,
They'd rise as one, their stories endure.

In the face of terror, they'd call out the abuser,
Demanding justice for innocence stolen, the accuser.
For in a world where victims are shamed and blamed,
A safe haven becomes a lifeline untamed.

FALSE WITNESSES

False witnesses they've become,
Crafting tales under the sun.
They claim to enforce discipline,
But behind closed doors, darkness looms.

Zero tolerance, they proudly proclaim,
For sexual misconduct, their empty fame.
Yet when questioned about their deeds,
They deny the truth, planting deceitful seeds.

Sexuality education seminars they declare,
Empowering students to speak out and share.
But when confronted with the reality,
They deny, deflect, and show no sincerity.

We asked them if a teacher had crossed the line,
Sexually harassing a student, a heinous crime.
They replied with confidence, a resounding "NEVER",
But in our hands, a suspension letter, a truth forever.

The evidence is clear, their words are untrue,
They hide the darkness that they once knew.
False witnesses, they stand in their charade,
Betraying trust, leaving victims betrayed.

How can we believe in their hollow façade,
When they deny the existence of the bad?
We must seek justice, expose their lies,
For the truth should never be compromised.

Let the voices of the victims rise,
Breaking the silence, shattering the disguise.
Hold them accountable, demand the truth,
Expose the false witnesses, uncloak their uncouth.

For the path to justice is paved with truth,
And falsehoods can never bring about its sooth.
Together, let us stand against the pretence,
And unveil the lies, restore the sense.

In that sacred space, free from judgment and scorn,
Victims find strength, their spirits reborn.
A place where healing can gently unfold,
Where scars can mend, where stories are told.

But in this world, where empathy is rare,
Where stigma surrounds, and justice seems unfair,
We must strive to build safe havens of care,
Where victims find solace, support beyond compare.

Together, let us shatter the walls of shame,
Embrace survivors, uplift their names.
For in their journey, we'll find the way,
To create a world where healing holds sway.

Let us forge a path of compassion and grace,
A safe haven where victims find their rightful place.
With empathy and understanding, hand in hand,
We'll build a future where healing will withstand.

WHAT A LOVING MAN

Oh, what a loving man you claim to be,
But your actions speak differently, you see.
A master of disguise, you wear,
Behind closed doors, a monster lurking there.

When will I learn to anticipate your rage,
To tread carefully and avoid your fiery stage?
I've been by your side for ages it seems,
Yet still, I'm caught in the web of your extreme.

Shouldn't I know by now, when you return,
That your anger will ignite, your fists will churn?
If only I could say the right words, do the right thing,
Then perhaps, I'd escape the pain your anger brings.

But foolish me, for thinking it's my fault,
That if I acted perfectly, your anger would halt.
No, a loving husband doesn't become a brute,
Turning his partner into a target to persecute.

Do you know how often I am driven mad?
By the chaos of your children, both good and bad?
Do you know the sacrifices I make, day by day,
Burning my fingers to ensure our happiness would stay?

Yet, in return, you repay my love with violence,
Inflicting pain and torment, a heartless defiance.
How can you call yourself a loving man,
When you make me a punching bag, not a fan?

It's time to break the chains, shatter the illusion,
I will find strength for a rightful resolution.
No more excuses, no more hiding behind false love,
I will put an end to this unending pain

WHO WILL?

Who will take stock of the food store,
And let me know when supplies run low?
Who will snuggle into my bed at night,
Reminding me that breathing is my right?

Who will look at me with innocent eyes,
And whisper sweet nothing into my ears?
Who will inspect the shoe rack, urging me to replace,
The worn-out pairs with fresh ones, a new embrace?

I cherish the warmth of your loving embrace,
As you cuddled me, filling my heart's empty space.
It pains me to know I won't be held that way,
But your brothers provide comfort, day by day.

Shaanah's artwork adorns the walls of my room,
A reminder of your presence, dispelling the gloom.
Naagh and Annagh, too, show their love so pure,
Together, we find solace, and strength to endure.

We all bear the weight of losing you, my dear,
But in each other, we find solace and cheer.
United, we'll navigate through this dreadful strife,
Surviving the horrors, together, in this life.

TIME FOR ACTION

In these sixteen days, we raise our voice,
Against gender-based violence, a haunting choice.
Declared by the UN, a call for change so clear,
But empty rhetoric echoes, a truth we must steer.

Year after year, officials make their plea,
To end the rape, to set the victims free.
Yet still, GBV rises, an alarming plight,
Talks fill the air, but no actions take flight.

When shall we decide, with resolute might,
To convict the abusers, to end this dark night?
No more letting them off, no more escape,
It's time for justice, to reshape our landscape.

In this activism, let our actions be the key,
To break the cycle, to set the victims free.
No more empty words, it's time to take a stand,
To protect and empower, to heal this wounded land.

BLOOD HOUNDS

In a land stained with blood, darkness prevails,
Carnivorous personalities, their evil trails.
A victim caught in their strife,
Imperialism clashes with neo-imperialist life.

A state teeters on the edge, hanging in despair,
As fear grips the land, leaving us aware,
Peace eludes us, slipping through our fingers,
In a nation consumed by conflict, anguish lingers.

First, Boko Haram emerged with its violent sway,
Spreading terror, seeking lives to slay.
Then came IPOB, adding to the fray,
Both driven by bloodlust, causing dismay.

Once known for its peace, a tranquil retreat,
Now a breeding ground for the deadliest feat.
These terror groups, hungry for bloodshed,
Unconcerned whose blood is freely shed.

In this land of turmoil, where chaos abound,
We yearn for solace, for peace to resound.
May the voices of reason rise above the fray,
To guide us towards a brighter, peaceful day.

Let us unite against violence and strife,
Working together to rebuild our lives.
With hope in our hearts and resilience in our souls,
We can overcome the darkness, achieve our goals.

For blood may be spilled, but it does not define,
The spirit of a nation, the strength that's mine.
In the face of adversity, we shall stand tall,
Resisting the call for violence, embracing peace for all.

BEYOND OUTRAGE

Beyond the outrage, they find strength,
In unity, in resilience, they go to any length.
Their fight is a beacon, a beacon of hope,
A call to action, a way to cope.

In the face of adversity, they remain unyielding,
Their hearts unwavering, their determination revealing.
For justice, they fight, for justice, they strive,
To protect the innocent, to keep dreams alive.

May their efforts bring change, a brighter tomorrow,
Where victims find solace, free from sorrow.
Beyond outrage, their mission endures,
To create a world where justice ensure.

SURVIVORS' SUPPORT

Survivors, strong, need understanding's embrace,
To speak their truth, to stand and face,
The shadows of abuse, the torment's cruel shout,
But sadly, they face a different, painful bout.

Those who should ensure justice's bright path,
Blame the victims, invoking victims' wrath.
Retraumatising wounds, the pain compounded,
Other survivors watching, their voices confounded.

The blame they carry, like a heavy weight,
Silencing their courage, sealing their fate.
But hear us now, victims are not weak,
They're silenced by insensitivity, a truth so bleak.

Bystanders and stakeholders, heed this plea,
Break the silence, set the victims free.
Survivors are strong, their voices to find,
Let's support and understand, be gentle and kind.

A CONSUMING FIRE

In twilight's dance of love and fear,
He shifts from gentle to severe.
A minute tender, the next stormy,
A love confessed, then rage so stormy.

As she dreams in tranquil repose,
Suddenly awoken, fear arose.
He looms above, a menacing tower,
Eyes aflame, a consuming fire.

In that moment, the embers spoke,
Threatening to her heart revoke.
To escape the fate statistics weave,
She knew, depart she must, and leave.

So, with courage, she chose flight,
From the tumult of the violent night.
In rhythms of resilience, she spun,
A tale of escape, a battle won.

MOVE ON

"Move on" these words they tell me
It's been one year
You have to let go
God has His reasons
He gives and He takes.
Move on
For the sake of the other kids
Move on
Be strong for them.

How do I move on?
Can someone tell me how please?
Yes, God has His reasons
Pray, can you beg Him to reveal them Please
The other kids, yes reason why I haven't crossed over.

Move on?
How do I forget part of the whole that made me
Laugh, sing and dance
Made me see the colors of life
That reminded me I had to breathe
That knew even when I did not
That I was short of oxygen.
How do I move on
When I still hear her cry for justice
How do I move on

With her crying for justice
Begging me not to allow any other child suffer her fate.

I am strong fighting for justice for Dido
I am strong for my boys
I am strong for the Naija child
I am strong fighting for the liberation of the countless Didos out there.

So please bear with me
When it seems, I am stuck
Pardon me
Please understand I am a grieving mother
Fighting for justice
Justice for a daughter that was sent to an early grave,

By those paid to care for her
A duty poorly delivered
Fighting to ensure history never repeats itself!
I will never be able to move on
But I promise I will learn to live with the pain.

- By Vivien Vihimga Akpagher (Late Keren's mother)

SILENTLY

Silently,
She left
Without a word spoken
She left
Shocked into silence
Her young mind stunned by the cruelty
Helpless as the builder's hammer broke her spirit
A citadel of learning turned into a house of horror
Words were not uttered
But marked Bible verses told a story word wouldn't have.

A broken hymen, laxed anal sphincter and a forgotten latex
Revealed pain the tongue was too heavy to reveal
Footages deleted covers betrayal by paid protectors
Samples retrieved in secrecy reveals corruption that reeks to high heavens
The deafening silence in government quarters, the elite protecting themselves
My dear, it's been a long year without you
I have stories to tell you someday
Stories weaved by management

And told by friends that know not the difference between betrayal and loyalty
Stories of elites, men and women that chose to stand with your oppressors.

Oh yes
But I also have stories of men and women of honour
That fought for justice for Keren
A society that called for accountability
Oh yes
I'll tell you all about it someday.

- By Vivien Vihimga Akpagher (Late Keren's mother)

www.ingramcontent.com/pod-product-compliance
Lightning Source LLC
LaVergne TN
LVHW041117150826
845673LV00007B/2090
9789787995235